Be kind.   "Create authentic power." ~Gary Zukav

"Take responsibility for your own well being." ~Brad Yates

Love always wins.

Say, "Thank-You"   "Refuse to sink." ~Denny Lewis

Your ego is not your amigo. ~Unknown

"Live your life in peace, not in pieces." ~Tyler Perry

One Step in Front of the Other

by Juanita Collins

Copyright © 2021 Juanita Collins
Book design by Tory Marshall

Published in 2021 by J.L. Collins. All rights reserved.
No portion of this book may be reproduced, stored in a retrieval system or transmitted in
any form or by means, mechanical, electronic, photography, recording, or otherwise,
without written permission from the publisher.

Library of Congress Cataloging-Publication Data available.
ISBN: 978-1-7379588-3-3

Printed in U.S.A.

Dedication

To YOU, my reader.
As you are reading this book right here, right now, know these words are for you.
Your life is a journey. Embrace every moment. Live the expected and unexpected.
Share. Know you are not alone.
You are loved.

To my North Star, soul mate, anchor, I love you Rafe.

And so it begins...

one step in front of the other.

As small babes, a gentle hand guides, leads, and protects.

One step

　　in front

　　　　of the other.

Growing, learning, dancing...
taking it all in.

Oh...oh!

A side step,

a trip, a fall;

not to worry...

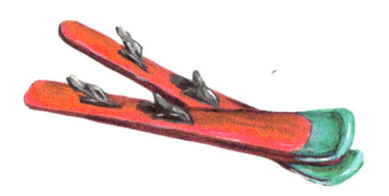

One step

    in front

        of the other.

As we continue on our path,

many join our circle.

Some stay, some linger, some move on.

One step

   in front

      of the other.

peeks and glows.

the runs, the losses.

One step

in front

of the other.

It's all part of the journey...
Breathe deeply.

Chin up;

never,

never,

give up!

Do so my friend,

with great courage and heart.

Acknowledgements

To Watts, Miske, and Schroeder; my soul sisters!
Thank you for your presence, guidance,
and lending ear.

Libbs, one of the most inspiring teachers I know.
The one who embraces the world of words.
Thank you.

To my island girl, Kristen. The talented graphic
designer who brings joy, and enthusiasm,
to every project. Mahalo.

To my beautiful, illustrator, Tory Marshall.
Your presence, grace, and gift has surpassed
the vision. Thank you for this incredible ride.
You're amazing!

To Gregg Brandalise, thank you, J.M. is smiling.

Tory Marshall, illustrator

San Diego based artist and published children's book illustrator, Tory Marshall, has contributed her paintings, drawings and mixed media work to the professional art world for over 15 years. While earning her degree in both studio art and art history, she discovered her deep passion for spreading awareness through conceptual painting. Tory has shared her expertise through her involvement in both local and international group and solo exhibitions. Her dedication to edification led her to teach art integration for the San Diego Unified School District, as well as conduct adult painting classes over the last 6 years. Her passion for community has inspired her involvement in a number of public projects, including orchestrating an urban arts initiative in Pohang, South Korea and the production of several recent murals in collaboration with the San Diego Museum of Art, Mindful Murals organization, SDG&E and local businesses in support of Black Lives Matter, Anti-AAPI Hate, and the LGBTQIA+ community.

Juanita Collins, author

Juanita Collins lives in Oceanside, CA with her husband of 35 years. When she's not writing, Juanita dabbles in the world of voice-over acting and enjoys eating all kinds of delicious chocolate while she pursues her passions of walking on the beach, dining with friends and family and traveling. Prior to becoming a published author, Juanita was a cast member at Disneyland for 15 years. She truly loved this job because not only is it "the happiest place on Earth", but it was also where she met her husband and made life-long friends. She went on to pursue her education at Cal State Long Beach and found her niche teaching young children how to read and become lifelong learners. She taught for 21 years in Carlsbad, CA where she was the recipient of prestigious Teacher of the Year award in 2010. "One Step in Front of the Other" is Juanita's debut picture book. This beautifully illustrated work captivates readers as it chronicles life as a process and a journey. When we slow down and take one step at a time, we are better able to navigate and embrace life's unlimited possibilities with grace and confidence. "One Step in Front of the Other" offers a poignant message not only for the young, but for all ages.

Printed in the USA
CPSIA information can be obtained
at www.ICGtesting.com
LVHW061355011023
759803LV00020B/851